Original title:
Life: One Big Cosmic Joke

Copyright © 2025 Creative Arts Management OÜ
All rights reserved.

Author: William Hawthorne
ISBN HARDBACK: 978-1-80566-021-7
ISBN PAPERBACK: 978-1-80566-316-4

To Laugh Among the Stars

In the grand circus of the sky,
Planets twirl and comets fly.
Stars wear hats, a silly sight,
As laughter echoes through the night.

Galaxies spin like clowns on stage,
Each black hole a comedic age.
Nebulas puff pink clouds of cheer,
While cosmic pranks bring smiles near.

Asteroids rolling, bumping heads,
Tickling moons, and cheeky spreads.
Supernova dances, bright and bold,
A cosmic jest that never gets old.

So let's toast with stardust wine,
To the quirks that intertwine.
In the universe, we play our part,
With giggles that light up the heart.

A Cosmic Tickle

Stars twinkle while planets spin,
A dance of chaos, where to begin?
Galaxies giggle in the dark night,
Whispers of humor in endless flight.

Time slips on a banana peel,
Wormholes stretch like a rubber meal.
Gravity's just a playful tease,
Holding us down with a cosmic breeze.

The Astral Comedy Club

In the universe's zany stage,
Stars tell jokes in a cosmic cage.
Black holes laugh in a swirling thread,
While comets crack up and leave us red.

Neutron stars with their ticklish cores,
Joke around with the force of wars.
Uranus grins with a pun so sly,
While Saturn rings in the midnight sky.

Comedic Cosmic Currents

Planets float on a sea of jest,
Sailing through space, we are but guests.
Meteorites like stand-up acts,
Crashing the atmosphere with laugh attacks.

Quantum quips in a particle dance,
Electrons play hide-and-seek by chance.
Time loops back for a second try,
As the universe chuckles, oh my my!

The Amusement Park of Atoms

Welcome to the fair of the unseen,
Rides of protons, crazy and keen.
Electrons swirl like children on swings,
Energized laughter as the cosmos sings.

The carousel spins with a neutron tune,
While helium balloons float near the moon.
Each atom a ride, swirling round and round,
In this jesting world, joy is found.

Constellations of Humor

Stars giggle in the night,
While comets dance in flight.
Galaxies spin with a grin,
As planets tease and spin.

Asteroids play tag on high,
Meteor showers wink and sigh.
Each twinkle tells a jest,
In this cosmic jesting fest.

Black holes swallow thoughts whole,
While neutron stars steal the show.
A supernova bursts with glee,
As laughter echoes in the spree.

In the vastness, jokes unfurl,
Creating chaos in a swirl.
For in the universe so wide,
Humor's always on the ride.

Weaving Laughter Through the Cosmos

Across the void, a chuckle roams,
Stitching nebulae into humorous tomes.
Saturn's rings spin tales so bright,
While Venus giggles in the soft twilight.

Planets wear hats made of dust,
In this tapestry, we trust.
Shooting stars deliver zany notes,
As stardust giggles from cosmic moats.

Quasars flash with a wink,
While superclusters pause to think.
Life's a tapestry of silly strings,
Woven tightly with cosmic flings.

In the grandeur, laughter weaves,
Among the tales, we dare believe.
Through the void and endless space,
Jokes carry us with such grace.

The Silly Symphony of Existence

In the orchestra of the skies,
Planets play with wide-eyed surprise.
The sun conducts with a radiant ray,
As stars harmonize in their own ballet.

Nebulas puff a colorful tune,
While black holes hum a joyful rune.
Galactic winds sweep the stage,
In this cosmic laughter, we engage.

Each quasar's pulse, a rhythm so bright,
Echoes the giggles of endless night.
Asteroids join in with a clang,
As the universe bursts into sang.

In this grand symphony we share,
Laughter echoes in cosmic air.
For in all the chaos, there's a song,
And their silly tunes keep us strong.

Juggling Planets and Punchlines

Planets juggle with effortless flair,
Tossing punchlines through the air.
Moons laugh as they spin around,
Creating giggles from the ground.

The sun cracks jokes in brilliant rays,
While darkness chuckles in mysterious ways.
Stars wink with mischievous glee,
In this cosmic circus, wild and free.

Asteroids tumble with comical flair,
Each one flinging laughter to share.
Galaxies collide in a humorous clash,
Turning seriousness into a flash.

In this dance of cosmic fun,
Every moment is a pun.
For amidst the chaos so divine,
Jokes make the universe align.

A Comedic Dance with Fate

In the theater of absurd, we prance,
With fate as our partner in this wild dance.
Tripping over banana peels with glee,
Floating on clouds of cotton candy spree.

The puppet strings tug, we're swayed by the breeze,
The universe chuckles, oh, what a tease!
We slip on rainbows and glide down the hill,
As laughter erupts, it's all quite a thrill.

The Canvas of Silly Spacetimes

On this canvas, galaxies spin and paint,
With brushstrokes of chaos, yet none are quaint.
Dancing in circles like toddlers in socks,
Juggling planets and laughing at clocks.

With stardust confetti, we party all night,
While comets do cartwheels, oh what a sight!
We scribble our dreams among cosmic art,
Each giggle and snicker, a beat of the heart.

Laughter Woven in Starlight

Starlit giggles echo far and wide,
As the cosmos watches, it cannot hide.
Galaxies chuckle in a whimsical loop,
While meteors crash in an interstellar scoop.

Shooting stars wink as they race across dark,
Tickling our spirits, igniting a spark.
Jokes fold like origami in the night sky,
Each chuckle a shimmer, a twinkling reply.

Cosmic Capers of Serendipity

In the great void, where time has no bounds,
Serendipity leaps, in laughter it resounds.
With twinkling eyes, we dance on the brink,
Comedic escapades make us rethink.

A mishap with gravity leads to a sigh,
Falling upwards, we joke as we fly.
The universe giggles, its humor so sly,
In cosmic capers, we're learning to try.

Comet's Comedic Journey

A comet streaked with flair and wit,
It danced through stars, a cosmic skit.
It waved to planets, laughed with glee,
In a universe that loves to be free.

With tails like ribbons, it flew on by,
Whispering jokes to the twinkling sky.
Asteroids chuckled, moons rolled their eyes,
As the comet spread joy in stellar skies.

Gleeful Galaxies

In swirling arms, the galaxies spun,
Each one a joker, each one a pun.
Stars wink in rhythm, planets burst out,
What a cosmic party, there's never a doubt!

Nebulas giggle, black holes tease,
Gravity's pull is no picnic, you see.
They chuckle and chortle across the night,
In this vast cosmos, laughter takes flight.

The Great Cosmic Riddle

What's a star's favorite type of game?
Why, it's a riddle, but never the same.
They twinkle and sparkle with puzzling cheer,
Inviting us all to lend them an ear.

In the dark of space, we ponder and muse,
While celestial bodies swap humorous views.
A quasar yells, "What's the punchline, friend?"
And the universe roars, 'There's no real end!'

Jests Across the Milky Way

Through the Milky Way, jokes travel fast,
From bright supernovae to shadows cast.
Star clusters chuckle, their beams aglow,
As they trade quips like pros, putting on a show.

A light-year's length is but a mere jest,
In this cosmic comedy, we're all a guest.
To giggles of stardust, we laugh and play,
On this wild ride, come join the fray!

A Comedian's View of Infinity

In a universe vast, we trip through the haze,
Chasing our tails in the most baffling ways.
Stars wink and chuckle at our endless plight,
As we fumble and stumble, a comic delight.

Black holes are jesters, swirling with glee,
Pulling in the wise and the not-so-free.
Planets spin round like a dizzying dance,
While comets just laugh at our fleeting chance.

Time ticks away, playing tricks with our minds,
A cosmic prankster, leaving humor that binds.
We search for the truth in quarks and in light,
Yet find only punchlines that spark and ignite.

So here's to the cosmos, a grand vaudeville show,
Where we're all just performers, putting on a flow.
With every missed cue and celestial blunder,
We giggle and grin through the cosmic wonder.

Cosmic Giggles and Galactic Grins

In galaxies bursting with cosmic confetti,
Stars are the party, and comets are petty.
Nebulas dance in a swirling ballet,
While black holes smirk at the mess we all play.

Laughter erupts from the Milky Way's core,
As planets make faces and tumble, explore.
The sun in the morning just can't help but beam,
While moons wink and nod, it's a whimsical dream.

Asteroids shout as they dodge and they weave,
While satellites gossip, it's hard to believe.
The universe chuckles, a jester so sly,
As we ponder our fate with a glint in our eye.

So let's raise a toast to this cosmic charade,
With every new twist that the cosmos has made.
For in this big circus, we find our delight,
In giggles and grins that stretch far into night.

Astronomical Absurdities

In the depths of the void where the absurdity dwells,
Galaxies twirl while a black hole repels.
Stars plummet down from their heavenly heights,
Just to join in on the universe's sights.

Jokes made of stardust and laughter ignite,
Asteroids tumble, their paths a pure fright.
While quasars quip at the speed of their light,
Making sense of it all? Well, that's not quite right.

The echo of laughter plays tricks on our ears,
As meteor showers dissolve all our fears.
Cosmic clowns float on the rings of a friend,
Grinning at us as they loop and they bend.

So let's not take gravity all too serious now,
For the universe's humor is eternal, somehow.
In this wild, wacky ride, take a seat, hold on tight,
The punchline's coming, just wait for the flight.

The Universe's Tongue-in-Cheek

Stars scatter jokes in a pitch-black expanse,
While planets spin tales in a dizzying dance.
Comets deliver their punchlines with style,
    As they whizz past in cosmic beguile.

The cosmos beholds with a cheeky delight,
Winking at mortals who ponder the night.
Between the dimensions, absurdity reigns,
In the fabric of space where laughter remains.

Time plays the fool, flipping seconds like coins,
While echoes of laughter drift through the joins.
Galactic comedians, both bold and quite spry,
Leave us in stitches as they zip through the sky.

So embrace the absurd, let your humor take flight,
In this vast, cosmic theater, we shine oh-so-bright.
For with every twist, turn, and cosmic surprise,
    A chuckle awaits in the grandest of skies.

The Silliness of Stardust

In a galaxy far away, so bright,
Planets twirled in sheer delight.
Stars winked like eyes in a jest,
While comets raced for a cosmic test.

Asteroids laughed as they rolled on by,
Making silly faces as they fly.
Black holes giggled, eating light,
In the vast expanse of the night.

Silly shadows danced on the moons,
To the rhythm of vibrating tunes.
Cosmic winds blew with a grin,
A big joke told in the silence within.

Even the sun burst into cheer,
Blasting solar flares, oh dear!
In the universe's wide embrace,
Laughter echoes through endless space.

The Quip of Cosmic Proportions

A star sneezed, and the dust did fly,
Creating planets with a sneezy sigh.
Galaxies spun with a punchline bright,
Jokes exchanged in the depths of night.

Nebulas painted with colors so wild,
As the universe giggled like a child.
Quasars blinked in a cheeky way,
Winking at comets on their playful sway.

Gravity tripped on a cosmic shoelace,
Astrophysicists scratching their face.
Space was witty, with humor to spare,
Laughter orbiting everywhere.

From stardust to the edge of the night,
Every twinkling light held a delight.
In the vastness, the punchlines chase,
Mirth and wonder fill every space.

The Playful Side of Space

Saturn wore rings just for show,
Spinning with flair, putting on a glow.
Mars cracked jokes with his dusty friends,
While cosmic laughter never ends.

Uranus chuckled at a stellar pun,
With swirling storms that danced and spun.
The Milky Way twirled in a jovial spree,
A galaxy of gags, wild and free.

Meteor showers, like confetti in flight,
Unraveled giggles in the cold night.
Stars threw parties with gleaming rays,
Celebrating life in curious ways.

Through black holes, they whispered and snickered,
As constellations played and flickered.
In this vast playground, a joyous maze,
Every twinkle shared in cosmic praise.

Infinite Jest Among the Stars

Out in the cosmos, where dreams align,
Stars tell jokes over a glass of wine.
They chuckle at time, watch it unwind,
In the vastness, humor's always kind.

Planets giggle as they spin around,
Sharing secrets without a sound.
Asteroids cracking up in their flight,
As space chuckles through the endless night.

Orion's belt, a twinkling nod,
Knows the jest is never flawed.
Laughter travels at light speed, you see,
In this universe, we're all just free.

Black holes pull in every last quip,
As comets race with a playful skip.
In the endless dance of cosmic jest,
The universe whispers, we are blessed.

Celestial Guffaws

Stars wink in the night,
Galaxies spin with cheer.
Planets dance in delight,
As comets turn and veer.

Gravity's silly pull,
Keeps us stuck to the ground.
But when we take a stroll,
It's irony we've found.

A black hole's big embrace,
Swallowing all it can find.
Yet it wears a funny face,
Leaving us in a bind.

The moon laughs and teases,
Eclipsed by its dark kin.
While the sun's bright sneezes,
Make day feel like a win.

The Universe's Trickster

Time ticks with a sly grin,
Winks at every little flaw.
It wraps us up in spin,
While we gape in awe.

Meteor showers rain,
As wishes float and fizzle.
Laughter echoes the pain,
Can't help but chuckle and drizzle.

Quantum leaps and bounds,
Make sense of the absurd.
In chaos, joy resounds,
Life's a cosmic wordbird.

Jesters in the sky,
Comets play peek-a-boo.
With cosmic laughter high,
Who needs a cue?

A Serenade of Cosmic Chuckles

Nebulas swirl in jest,
Tickling our dreams so bright.
Every dream's a quest,
Hitch a laugh all night.

Galactic pranks parade,
Orbits twirl in a wink.
Even black holes are made,
To make us stop and think.

Asteroids bob and weave,
With a shimmery a-woo.
Funny tunes they leave,
While dancing in the blue.

Cosmic melodies play,
In the theater of space.
With humor guiding the way,
What a joyous race!

Joy in the Cosmic Theater

Stars perform their grand show,
Each twinkle a line well-rehearsed.
With space as their stage glow,
Every burst is well-versed.

Planets spin in a jest,
Their orbits a goofy dance.
Audiences gasp in the fest,
Marveling at sheer chance.

Laughter echoes so wide,
As asteroids make their rounds.
Every bump is a ride,
In this comedy of sounds.

So let's toast to the night,
Raise our cups to the skies.
For in the cosmic light,
Humor forever lies.

Satirical Stardust

In a universe where chaos reigns,
Stars collide, as laughter gains.
Planets trip upon their orbits,
Cosmic puns fly like comets.

Gravity's just a heavyweight's joke,
As if the moon's a cosmic bloke.
Slipping through each wormhole's snare,
We tumble through, with naught a care.

Asteroids wear their finest hats,
While galaxies dance, just like spats.
Nebulae knit their bright shawls,
Amidst the laughter of space's calls.

So here we spin, with arms held wide,
In this absurdity, we take pride.
Stars are just candles flickering bright,
In the cosmic jest of day and night.

The Grand Cosmic Spoof

Oh, the universe plays tricks so sly,
With comet tails that wave goodbye.
Black holes swallow every last snack,
While nova bursts send joy off track.

Alien life just makes us grins,
Spacetime's fabric wears and thins.
Supernovae clap with glee,
As planets spin in parody.

Eclipses peek from behind the sun,
Jokes in the cosmos, oh what fun!
Constellations giggle in the dark,
Drawing silly shapes, a cosmic lark.

With each pulsar's heart giving a beat,
We join the dance, our fate is sweet.
In this grand cosmic circus, we play,
Waving to stars that twinkle and sway.

Cosmic Gags and Giggles

Galaxies twirl in a clumsy waltz,
Creating wonders, yet never halts.
Quasars make the best of their day,
With punchlines bright, they light the way.

Asteroids laugh as they zoom past Mars,
Trading jokes with the shimmering stars.
Silly comets with tails that sweep,
Whispering secrets as they leap.

Time bends over in fits of cheer,
While we try to guess what's over here.
With every orbit, there's something new,
A mirthful spark in the grand cosmic brew.

So let's toast to our cosmic fate,
In this grand theater, we narrate.
Each twinkle and spin a jest so sly,
Under the watchful cosmic eye.

The Absurdity of Celestial Being

Whispers of the cosmos, oh so wry,
Planets parade in the endless sky.
Quirky moons that laugh on the side,
In this heaven, we chuckle with pride.

Time loops around like a playful kitten,
As stars wink, their light has bitten.
Wormholes giggle with every breach,
Telling tales they love to teach.

Gravity's pull, a sneaky swipe,
As orbits ebb and flow, oh ripe!
From black holes to the bright sun's glow,
Eccentricities reshape the flow.

In an absurd dance, we spin and sway,
Finding joy in the random fray.
For in this grand scheme, we often find,
A cosmic joke has us entwined.

Cosmic Punchlines in the Stars

In cosmic halls, the stars do giggle,
As planets dance and comets wiggle.
Black holes snicker, making a fuss,
While shooting stars shout, "Ride the bus!"

Galaxies spin, their humor grand,
Creating jokes no one can understand.
Even the moons can't help but to cheer,
As echoes of laughter float far and near.

Laughter at the End of the Universe

At the edge of time, a joke is spun,
The universe grins; oh, isn't it fun?
Planets colliding, like two old pals,
Leaving stardust trails and comical sprawls.

Quasars quip, oh, what a delight,
As time ticks on, they share their light.
Gravity binds us, yet brings such cheer,
In this cosmic game, we find our beer.

The Comedy of Existence

Existence winks, a trickster in space,
With punchlines that leave us lost in grace.
Atoms collide in a laughable spree,
Creating chaos, don't take it seriously!

Chaotic vibes in the nebula's sway,
Tickling souls in a playful ballet.
Even the asteroids laugh as they roll,
In this grand act, we're all part of the whole.

Jests Beneath the Celestial Canopy

Beneath the stars, a joke is told,
With every twinkle, the story unfolds.
Cosmic jesters in their gleaming attire,
Fueling our dreams, igniting our fire.

In twilight's glow, the universe preens,
As galaxies giggle in outrageous scenes.
With every sunrise, the laughter grows wide,
In this humorous journey, let's enjoy the ride.

Ticklish Tides of Time

Waves of laughter wash ashore,
Tickles in the cosmic score.
Stars above just wink and say,
'Join the dance, come out and play!'

Every moment, a jest divine,
Juggling time with a comic line.
Fate pulls pranks, then hides away,
While we giggle, in disarray.

Life's a joke wrapped in a riddle,
Chasing dreams, we strum the middle.
In the blink, we're up, then down,
From joyful cheers to silly frowns.

So here's to chaos, laughter bright,
In absurdity, we find delight.
Ride the waves, let humor flow,
In ticklish tides, we laugh and glow.

The Farce of Existence

A puppet show upon the stage,
Each player wears a laughter gauge.
With punchlines aimed at fate's own face,
We bow and smile, embracing grace.

Silly hats and goofy tunes,
The cosmos dances with cartoon moons.
Each day's a sketch, a colorful spree,
Painting absurdity for all to see.

We stumble into life's next scene,
Tripping over what might have been.
Yet with a chuckle, we rise anew,
For the farce delights, it's all true blue.

So raise a toast to cosmic jest,
In this play, we are all blessed.
To laughter loud and giggles sly,
Let's revel 'neath the endless sky.

Hello from the Other Side

Echoes from beyond the veil,
Whispering tales of our grand fail.
'Hey down there, you silly crew,
Your jokes are bright, your skies so blue!'

Time zones play a tricky game,
What's out there, we'll never tame.
Yet here we are, a cosmic chat,
Life's a clown, and we're the brat.

With every hiccup, snort, and giggle,
We shake the stars and make them wiggle.
From astral planes, they cheer and sing,
'Bravo, humans! Dance and swing!'

So here's a wink from the unknown,
Each laugh a seed, brightly sown.
We wave from here to realms so wide,
'Hello, dear friends, from the other side!'

Cosmic Laugh Tracks

A universe filled with roars and cheers,
Echoing through the void, teasing fears.
With every blip, every twist and turn,
A soundtrack plays—our hearts do yearn.

Glimmers of humor in starlit nights,
Casting shadows, igniting lights.
We ride the waves of cosmic blend,
In every giggle, we transcend.

The aftershocks of a comet's tear,
Shake the ground; we jump, we share.
Every joke written in the stars,
Perplexing minds from Earth to Mars.

With each chuckle, the heavens sing,
Reminding us of the joy we bring.
So tune in close, hear the tracks align,
In the cosmic jest, we're all just fine.

The Chuckling Cosmos

Stars twinkle like they know a joke,
Planets dance, in circles they poke.
Gravity plays its trickster role,
While comets streak, on a whim they stroll.

A moonbeam slips, and lands on a cat,
It blinks, confused, then gives a spat.
Black holes giggle, swirling around,
In this vast ball, absurdity's found.

Cosmic dust, with a wink and a grin,
Spills secrets of where to begin.
Time passes with a playful tease,
As constellations wear mismatched keys.

Smiles Beneath the Celestial Dome

Under the stars, a crowd made of light,
Gathers for jokes, oh what a sight!
Planets whisper their tales of folly,
While asteroids laugh in riotous jolly.

Shooting stars race, but trip on air,
Their friends chuckle—"Such grace, I swear!"
Galaxies spin, with giggles they blend,
In this grand show, there's no need to mend.

Comets with tails, waving hi,
Distracting the moon, who's lost in the sky.
Every bounce, a wink, a nudge,
As cosmic travelers wouldn't begrudge.

The Universe's Laughing Matter

In a galaxy far, over the hill,
Laughter echoes, quite a thrill.
Quasars stutter, pulsars beam bright,
As they trade puns under cosmic light.

Nebulae swirl with colors that jest,
"Look at me!" they giggle, always the best.
Synchronicity winks, stars take a bet,
On who'll trip first; no signs of regret.

Asteroids bicker—a playful dispute,
While black holes snicker, 'Is that a hoot?'
Supernovae dance, throw parties for free,
For the universe knows, it's all meant to be.

Cosmic Follies

Planets wobble, trying to stand,
While suns crack jokes, so perfectly planned.
Asteroids tumble, their balance askew,
In the theater of space, the slapstick ensues.

From the tail of a comet to the belt of a star,
Every twist and turn, laughter travels far.
The universe grins with a cosmic tease,
As laughter drifts through stardust and breeze.

Even black holes have their comedic days,
Pulling in matter, to fuel their plays.
Between the stars, absurdity roams,
In this vast place, there's always room for 'home'.

Whispers of the Infinite

In the cosmic dance, we twirl and spin,
Clumsy steps bring laughter, oh, where to begin?
Planets collide with a chuckle and cheer,
Tickling the void, we wander, no fear.

A comet slips by, dressed in sparkly flair,
"Watch me!" it screams, as it tumbles through air.
Galaxies grunt in a stellar parade,
Cosmic antics, a joke well-played.

Wormholes giggle as they stretch and tease,
"Come take a ride," they say with such ease.
Time trips on itself, falls flat on its face,
Tickles the edges of space, what a race!

So here we are, in the great cosmic jest,
Finding our punchlines, we strive for the best.
With each silly plummet, trip, and surprise,
The universe chuckles, a wink in its eyes.

Stars in Stitches

The stars are snickering, winking in the night,
Twinkling like mad, oh, what a delight!
"Can you believe it?" they whisper and glow,
"Look at those mortals, marching below!"

A black hole grins, with a mischievous spin,
Sucking up laughter, where to begin?
Singularities chuckle, they're full of surprise,
Gravity's punchline brings tears to our eyes.

The sun cracks a joke about burning too bright,
"Here's a tip, don't stare, it's quite the fright!"
Planets roll over, in orbit they lie,
Spinning through humor, in the cosmic sky.

So float on through space, with a grin on your face,
Embrace the absurd, it's a wonderful place.
For in this great cosmos, with laughter, we blend,
A tapestry woven, with giggles at the end.

The Comedic Veil of Existence

Behind the curtain, the show's just begun,
Existence a farce, but oh, what fun!
Jokes populating the fabric of time,
With punchlines that echo, rhythm and rhyme.

The universe winks, it's a playful affair,
Stars in their corners, just giggling out there.
Black holes whisper secrets, oh, what a sight,
While quasars burst forth, shooting jokes in the night.

Cosmic clowns dance on the ring of a star,
"Did you hear the one about how near we are?"
Asteroids chuckle, their paths filled with glee,
Bumping and bouncing, their own comedy spree.

So let's join the laughter, the silly and strange,
In this cosmic theater, where we rearrange.
With joy we embrace, what a riot it seems,
For the punchline of existence is woven with dreams.

Humorous Echoes of Eternity

Eternity hums with a whimsical tone,
Echoes of laughter, like seeds that are sown.
Time trips on its shoelaces, round and round,
In the comedy club, where stardust is found.

The moons juggle planets with a chuckle and spin,
"Watch this!" they cheer, as they all tumble in.
Galactic giggles bounce off the night,
Filling the void with a soft, joyous light.

A dance of the atoms, a jig in the void,
Creating connections, in laughter, deployed.
So let's tumble through moments, both silly and true,
In the comedy of cosmos, for me and for you.

For every bright spark, there's a joke to unfold,
Wrap yourself in the warmth, let the stories be told.
In the laughter of ages, we find our own way,
Eternity beams with a grin every day.

Eternal Whimsy of the Night Sky

Stars wink and giggle up high,
Moon chuckles as it passes by.
Galaxies spin in a silly dance,
Comets race with a gleeful glance.

Planets play hide and seek at night,
Jupiter wears a crown so bright.
Saturn's rings just love to tease,
While cosmic winds whisper with ease.

Asteroids tumble in playful spins,
Cosmic dust is where humor begins.
In this vast theater beyond our sight,
Every twinkle invites us to delight.

So gaze above, let laughter reign,
For in the cosmos, joy's our gain.
With each breath of the starlit air,
We find the humor floating everywhere.

A Dance of Shadows and Jests

In the corner, shadows prance,
With silly hats, they take their chance.
Whispers in the dark conspire,
To light a spark of pure desire.

Laughter echoes against the wall,
Ghosts of giggles softly call.
The clock ticks in a bouncy beat,
Time itself joins this playful feat.

As moonbeams shimmy through the trees,
They tickle leaves, tease the breeze.
A jest of dusk and dawn entreated,
Where every moment feels completed.

So twirl in shadows, dance away,
With every jest, we'll seize the day.
In this grand spectacle of fun,
We find the jokes, shared by everyone.

Nebulae of Nuance

Clouds of color swirl and play,
In the universe's grand ballet.
Particles giggle, stardust beams,
Crafting chaos from our dreams.

Whirls of gas in a cosmic twirl,
Spinning tales with every swirl.
Each nebula, a canvas wide,
Of whimsy lost in the cosmic tide.

Colors clash, a vibrant spree,
Creating surprises for you and me.
As science laughs, theories collide,
In this playful universe, we abide.

So let your worries drift afar,
In the vastness, we're the stars.
With laughter bright across the span,
Join the dance, oh, cosmic fan!

The Amusing Allure of the Unknown

Hidden corners of the vast unseen,
Crack jokes beneath the stars' sheen.
Each mystery sings, giggles out loud,
In the realm of shadows, we're avowed.

Bold explorers dive into the deep,
Where truth wears a mask, secrets keep.
Every riddle holds a playful sigh,
Stretched across the endless sky.

In this uncharted territory dance,
Where logic falters, dreams entrance.
With every question, laughter swells,
Witty tales the universe tells.

So venture forth, embrace the jest,
In uncertainty, we find our best.
For in the unknown's playful role,
We dance with joy, that's the goal.

The Paradox of Giggles

In a world where socks go missing,
We laugh at all the twists and turns.
The cat who thinks he's in charge,
While dancing on the table, he yearns.

A slip on a banana peel, oh what glee,
The way we trip through each bright day.
With every fall, a chuckle shares,
The joy inside the silly fray.

We ponder why the sun won't stay,
Yet chase the moon as it plays around.
A cosmic dance of mischief bright,
In laughter's web, we're tightly bound.

With grins held tight, we carry on,
In paradox we find our way.
A punchline here, a wink up there,
In giggles, we embrace the play.

Existence's Joking Heart

With every tick, the clock will tease,
As we scramble through the endless race.
We try to catch a fleeting breeze,
Yet tumble down without a trace.

A chicken crossed the road, they say,
But never reached the other side.
In silliness, we find our way,
The cosmic joker full of pride.

The bread we toast always lands spread,
With butter on the floor, how grand!
We laugh at jokes that dance in head,
A fortune cookie by our hand.

So raise a glass to every plight,
To laughter's spark when skies are gray.
For in this game of day and night,
We wear our joy like a bouquet.

Twists of the Cosmic Sideshow

Step right up to see the show,
Where planets spin like plates on poles.
A circus of stars that ebb and flow,
Their twinkling lights ignite our souls.

A jester's hat upon a sun,
As comets race in wild delight.
We laugh at all the battles won,
In cosmic jest, both day and night.

The universe plays peek-a-boo,
With black holes and their secret tricks.
A riddle wrapped in something new,
As laughter sparkles, time just ticks.

So here we stand, clowning our fate,
In every twist, we find our cheer.
With stardust cloaked, we celebrate,
The sideshow on this cosmic sphere.

Jokes Written in Starlight

In skies above, the punchlines glow,
As comets curl with witty grace.
The universe, a grand show,
With humor stitched in starry lace.

A giggle here, a chuckle there,
As meteor showers drop their quips.
We toss our cares into the air,
And catch the laughter on our lips.

A wormhole skirts a cosmic jest,
As time and space play silly games.
With cosmic tides that never rest,
Each joke an echo in our flames.

So here we dance beneath the light,
With jokes inscribed in endless night.
For in the universe's embrace,
We find our joy, our funny place.

The Amusing Paradox of Existence

We're all just players on a stage,
Stumbling through this comical age.
With scripts written in invisible ink,
We laugh and then we simply blink.

Chasing dreams on a merry-go-round,
Falling up when we should touch ground.
Riding waves of the wild and absurd,
In this circus, every thought is stirred.

Juggling troubles that seem so grand,
While rubber chickens fill our hands.
Expecting wisdom from seasoned fools,
We march along while breaking rules.

In the end, with humor we cope,
Finding giggles, the ultimate hope.
Around each corner, a chuckle we find,
Tickled by truths that life leaves behind.

Celestial Jokers

Stars wink down, a mischievous glow,
Spinning tales that we barely know.
The universe laughs at our plans,
Dancing in orbit, oh how it spans!

Planets chuckle as they sway,
In this cosmic game, we play all day.
Chasing comets with our open minds,
While black holes snicker, leaving us blind.

Galaxies giggle, their arms entwine,
Timeless jokes in a heavenly design.
Eclipses tickle, shadows at play,
In this vast void, who needs dismay?

From meteors flying, to the comets' tails,
Life is a joke, filled with giggles and gales.
So let's toast to the stars, and their whimsy ways,
In this cosmic circus, we're here for the praise.

Laughing at the Infinite Void

In the silence where echoes roam,
We find our laughter, calling it home.
Cosmic whispers tickle our ears,
While dark matter swirls around our fears.

The void winks back, a jesting friend,
Promising chaos, but not the end.
Stars break out in a twinkling dance,
As we stumble in our cosmic trance.

We trip on the edges of fate's grand design,
Roaming through shadows, sipping on wine.
Gravity giggles as we float and sink,
In the grand scheme, we pause to think.

Embracing the mischief beyond the scope,
Boldly we wander, tied by our hope.
So here's to the void, with its riotous charms,
As we roam through its laughter, wrapped in its arms.

The Laughter of Lost Planets

Once orbs of joy, now drifting far,
Whispering secrets from a dying star.
In cosmic corners, they giggle aloud,
Joking about their own oblivious crowd.

Eons of silence, then bursts of mirth,
Celebrating their not-so-glorious birth.
With rings of laughter and moons as jest,
They tell us it's all just a cosmic quest.

Comets pass by with a teasing grin,
Reminding us of the chaos within.
As we spin through space, a wild ballet,
These lost planets jest in their peculiar way.

So join the dance, let your worries sway,
In the laughter of planets, we find our play.
For what's the point of this grand cosmic plot,
If we can't share smiles, after all, why not?

Whims of the Universe

Galaxies dance in a silly waltz,
Stars twinkle like they're having a ball.
Planets trip over cosmic faults,
While black holes just laugh at it all.

Asteroids skate on ice made of dust,
Comets blow kisses, oh what a fling.
The universe giggles, it's perfectly just,
As it spins us around on a dramatic string.

Time jumps around, a real funny act,
Yesterday's future is always delayed.
Gravitational pulls make us lose track,
As we're wrapped in this cosmic charade.

Light years stretch with a wink and a nod,
While we search for meaning in space's grand play.
The universe chuckles at each little prod,
Reminding us all to just laugh at the sway.

Cosmic Punchlines

What did the stardust tell the moon?
'You're looking a bit out of phase!'
Stars take bets on which one will swoon,
As comets laugh in their glowing rays.

A dying star's joke fell quite flat,
As it tried to ignite one last spark.
But black holes chuckled, 'Look at that!
It spiraled down—what a cosmic lark!'

Aliens ponder, 'What's the point here?'
As they scan our quirks from afar.
They chuckle and sip on a soft cosmic beer,
While we train our eyes on the stars.

Among the nebulae, chuckles abound,
Understanding all of our silly mistakes.
The universe nods at the laughter we found,
"In the grand scheme, it's all just a break!"

Laughter Among the Stars

In the rhythm of orbits, a giggle can soar,
Planets spin tales as they loop and they weave.
Meteor showers that cause us to roar,
While we tumble in stardust, it's hard to believe.

Constellations wink, sharing secrets unspun,
While black holes whisper, 'Come on, take a ride!'
Space is a stage, and we're all in for fun,
As we orbit around with our arms open wide.

The galaxies chuckle when we start to plot,
They know our plans aren't a piece of the game.
In this cosmic circus, we give all we've got,
With laughter combined, what a beautiful shame!

Supernovae burst, a party ensues,
As the cosmos delights in its radiant show.
The universe teases with nothing to lose,
In the laughter of stars, joy continues to flow.

The Jester's Playbook

The universe scripts with a quirk in its plot,
Stars scribble punchlines while planets collide.
In the game of existence, hilarity's sought,
As we dance through the cosmos with laughter as guide.

Here's to the jester with a cosmic jest,
Who plays on the strings of the vast, endless night.
Each galaxy's giggle is simply the best,
In the chaos of space, what a dish of delight!

Astrological markers point to the wise,
Yet truth bounces back like a rubber band.
Humor's the secret, the grand cosmic prize,
That slips through our fingers like soft, gentle sand.

And as we rewind in the celestial haze,
The jester ensures we get lost in the fun.
For the quirks of the universe earn hearty praise,
As we laugh in the face of the race we've just run.

Cosmic Ironies and Celestial Shenanigans

Stars twinkle bright, yet we're lost in the fray,
Comets dance by, leading us astray.
We seek wisdom in the vast, empty dark,
Finding answers in the light of a spark.

Planets spin round, in a dance quite absurd,
As we ponder life's questions, rarely heard.
The universe chuckles, a giggle so grand,
While we build our castles in shifting sand.

Black holes are portals, or so we suppose,
But they swallow our dreams like a cosmic prose.
Each wish like a stardust, floating away,
Lost in the humor of night turning to day.

So raise up your glass to the cosmic display,
Where irony reigns, come what may.
In this galactic circus, we play our small part,
With laughter and joy that resides in the heart.

Laughter Echoing in the Silence

In the vacuum of space, a joke's on repeat,
Echoes of laughter, they dance to the beat.
Galaxies giggle, their spirals a tease,
As we float in the void, like dust in the breeze.

Meteor showers, a comedy show,
Wishes erupt like popcorn: 'To the stars we'll go!'
Yet every new leap feels just like a slip,
Tripping on stardust, oh what a trip!

Aliens ponder our curious plight,
With telescopes trained on our struggles at night.
"What's that down there? A big cosmic jest?"
While we search for meaning, they're humor-obsessed.

So chuckle along as the cosmos spins round,
Each twist and each turn is hilariously sound.
In laughter we find the glue that connects,
In the serene silence, humor reflects.

Galaxies of Guffaws

From spinning orbits to quirky old quarks,
The universe revels, igniting its sparks.
Jokes that eclipse us and comments that sting,
In the vastness of night, let the giggles take wing.

Life's a wild ride on a celestial train,
Where planets collide and forget to complain.
Gravity's pull, a mischievous grin,
As we tumble through time, let the laughter begin.

Nebulas tease with colors so bright,
Riddles unravel in the stillness of night.
Comedic endeavors in the starry expanse,
A universe laughing, inviting us to dance.

So gather your stardust and join in the mirth,
For humor's a treasure, a cosmic rebirth.
In the play of existence, the punchline must land,
As galaxies giggle, we stand hand in hand.

Quirky Quarks and Cosmic Capers

Quarks jive and jolt in a whimsical spree,
While photons play tag, 'Come out to see!'
Cosmic capers unfold with each twinkling star,
Who knew the universe could be this bizarre?

A supernova's burst is a glitzy surprise,
Like confetti of stars that bursts from the skies.
Atoms all chuckle as they swirl in delight,
Building the universe deep into the night.

Electrons misbehave, causing chaos and cheer,
While atoms engage in a game of idea.
Black holes are punchlines we struggle to see,
Sucking in jokes and the laughter of glee.

So tip your hat to the cosmic ballet,
Where humor's the force in this grand cabaret.
In the theater of space, we play our small role,
With quirky quarks leading to joy in the soul.

Cosmic Ironies

Stars twinkle high in the sky,
Yet we're stuck here asking why.
With gravity holding us down,
We still laugh, wearing our crown.

Planets spin in their own dance,
While we trip, miss our chance.
Galaxies stretch, far and wide,
But we can't find a place to hide.

Comets blaze like a shooting star,
But that won't get us very far.
In the chaos, there's delight,
As we fumble through the night.

What's the punchline to this show?
We might never really know.
But humor's the glue that keeps us whole,
In this cosmic, rollicking stroll.

A Cosmic Stand-Up

Why did the asteroid cross the void?
To find that space was just a ploy!
Punchlines span solar arrays,
In the echoes of cosmic bays.

Saturn's rings, a glittering bind,
Are great for a laugh, but never kind.
On Jupiter's storms, we toss our fate,
While aliens giggle at our state.

Stars tell tales of celestial pranks,
As we balance on life's overdrawn blanks.
"Knock, knock!" says the Milky Way,
"Who's there?"—Just another day!

Stand-up routines of the universe,
Leave us in stitches, yet we rehearse.
For with every quirk and twist of fate,
We share a laugh while we navigate.

Quirky Quasars

Quasars blink like winking eyes,
In the backdrop of endless skies.
They whisper secrets on cosmic winds,
Of all the mischief the universe spins.

A neutron star's eccentric spin,
Is just like us trying to fit in.
And black holes munching on old stars,
Remind us not to take things too far.

Light-years away, the jokes unfold,
As we chase dreams we dare to hold.
Through the comets with tails like kites,
We find humor in the cosmic flights.

The heavens giggle, what a sight!
With cosmic chuckles to ignite.
In the end, it's all just fun,
The universe knows how to run!

The Universe's Absurd Tales

In the vacuum, where silence reigns,
Absurdities weave curious chains.
A star sneezes, a comet blinks,
While we ponder what life thinks.

Shooting stars are just cosmic pranks,
Playing tricks in celestial ranks.
Aliens laugh, with eyes wide,
As we trip on this wild ride.

Black holes hide the punchline well,
Swallowing jokes we cannot tell.
In every blink and every twirl,
There's a chuckle waiting to unfurl.

With every leap through space and time,
Absurdity jingles like a chime.
So let's embrace this wacky stroll,
In a universe that loves to cajole.

Whimsical Wandering Through Infinity

In the dance of dust and stars,
We chase our tales on cosmic bars.
Each twinkle winks a playful tease,
As planets swirl with global ease.

Laughter echoes through the void,
Where serious thoughts are oft destroyed.
A comet slips upon banana peels,
While Saturn spins and space-time squeals.

With every giggle in the sky,
A black hole's wink makes starlings fly.
Oh, what a circus, bright and wild!
The universe laughs, a carefree child.

So grab your dreams and float away,
On cosmic waves where jesters play.
In infinity's embrace, we glide,
Through whimsy's realm, our souls abide.

The Grin of the Celestial Court

In the court of stars, a jester beams,
With galaxies swirling in comic themes.
A crown of comets upon his head,
Sowing laughter where starlight's spread.

Nebulas chuckle, dressed in hue,
While solar winds tickle every view.
Laughing moons spin a tale so grand,
As solar flares wave a playful hand.

Each black hole hides a playful jest,
A cosmic riddle in the celestial nest.
Asteroids roll like marbles tossed,
In the game of time, most happily lost.

Thus in this court, beneath cosmic light,
We celebrate the day and night.
For every twinkle holds a grin,
As universal humor dances in.

Starry-Eyed Satire

With starlit eyes, we gaze around,
At antics of the universe found.
A supernova, in jest, ignites,
While space-time bends in playful flights.

Galaxies giggle, each swirl a joke,
As meteors flash and planets evoke.
A starlet fluffs her fiery plume,
Casting shadows in the cosmic bloom.

The asteroid's path is a stumble and trip,
As comic relief takes a cosmic dip.
Mirth in the chaos, a twist in the tale,
Where gravity bows and laughter prevails.

So toast to the cosmos, a humor divine,
In every quasar, the truth we align.
For while we may ponder the vast and unknown,
The universe giggles, never alone.

The Universe's Comic Opera

On the grandest stage, the stars collide,
In this opera where the comets glide.
Each note a spark, each beat a twirl,
As galaxies whirl in a dazzling swirl.

The planets audition for cosmic fame,
While meteors crash like a wild game.
Nebulas sing with colors bright,
As stardust dances in sheer delight.

The moon, a diva, in silvery light,
Pulls at the tides with playful might.
A cosmic orchestra plays its score,
While quarks and leptons shout for more!

So join the chorus in this vast space,
Every heartbeat a laugh, every grace.
In the universe's theater, we play our part,
With humor stitched deep in the cosmic heart.

The Celestial Circus

Planets tumble, stars collide,
Galaxies twist, oh what a ride!
A comet slips, it takes a fall,
As laughter echoes through it all.

A ringmaster winks, the moon takes flight,
Juggling meteors, what a sight!
Black holes joke, they spin and twirl,
In this cosmic show, watch it unfurl.

Saturn's rings, a clown's red nose,
While solar flares burst out in prose,
Each cosmic act, a sight to see,
In this great circus, wild and free.

Laughing stars wink from far above,
Tickling our hearts, spreading the love,
Join the dance in the stellar spree,
In the celestial circus, come and be!

Humorous Horizons

Clouds tickle the sun as they pass,
While rainbows giggle in the grass,
Each horizon grins, a cheeky tease,
Whispers of joy dance in the breeze.

Mountains chuckle, valleys respond,
Echoing jokes of the distant pond,
Stars shine brightly with cheeky glee,
As comets crack jokes, wild and free.

Laughter rings out from every shore,
While waves embrace the sandy floor,
Horizons stretched like a giant grin,
As the universe invites us in.

In this vast realm of whimsy grand,
Where time is fickle, like shifting sand,
Join the laughter, let worries cease,
In humorous horizons, find your peace.

The Joyous Identity Crisis of Stars.

Stars ponder deep who they might be,
A sun with a job or a wild sea?
Twinkling bright, seeking to shine,
Yet every night, they lose that line.

"Am I a planet? Am I a moon?"
Sing one to another, in cosmic tune,
Each has a story, yet all feel lost,
In the twinkling chaos, what's the cost?

Supernovae burst, then giggle away,
"I'm a fireworks show! Come, watch me play!"
While black holes swirl, with mystery vast,
"Who knew being dark could be such a blast?"

In this stellar riddle, they find their spark,
As cosmic jesters in the cosmic dark,
A joyful crisis, who could resist?
The stars just laugh — they truly exist!

The Universe's Witty Whisper

The stars wink low with a secret shared,
Whispers of humor, tones unpaired,
Galaxies spin, like jokes take flight,
In the silence of space, there's pure delight.

Nebulae giggle in vibrant hues,
Painting the cosmos with playful views,
Each comet streaks by, a punchline's grace,
In the grand joke of this endless space.

Cosmic echoes shout, "Can you believe?"
As stardust chuckles, the night takes leave,
A universe packed with witticism bright,
In every twinkle, a spark of light.

So listen closely, join the jest,
For in this expanse, we're truly blessed,
In the universe's quirky whisper, we find,
A shared laughter, forever entwined.

Cosmic Chuckles in the Void

In the vastness where dreams collide,
Stars winking like they know the tide,
Comets trail off with a teasing zoom,
While planets giggle in their merry gloom.

Galaxies twirl in a dizzy way,
Spinning tales of night and day,
Black holes burp and swallow light,
A cosmic jest, what a silly sight!

The universe shrugs, a knowing grin,
Making mischief where we've been.
Nebulas burst in cotton candy hues,
Confetti of chaos, what fun to choose!

So here we float in our tiny speck,
Dressed in fate's most awkward peck,
In this grand show of cosmic play,
We're all just laughs in the Milky Way.

Punch Drunk on Stardust

Waking up with a cosmic hangover,
Stars above me dance and hover,
Sipping dreams through a silver straw,
Giggling softly at the cosmic law.

Asteroids fall like confetti bright,
While meteors make a stunning flight,
Each tumble telling a story bold,
Of cosmic clowns and space-time gold.

The moon winks down with a cheeky smile,
Saying, 'Just stick around for a while,'
Dancing to the tune of celestial pranks,
In this wild cosmos of sordid flanks.

Here we sway, a drunken affair,
Bathed in stardust, without a care,
So grab a laugh, it's quite a tease,
In this universe, we take our ease.

A Riddle Wrapped in Starlight

The cosmos whispers secrets untold,
Dancing shadows, bright and bold,
With riddles tucked in every beam,
Joking softly through a cosmic dream.

Where black holes swallow what they find,
And stars hold hands, forever entwined,
Each twinkle hides a playful jest,
In the vault of space, we're all guests.

Time spins tales in a silly way,
Laughing as we bob and sway,
In this riddle wrapped in starlight,
We stumble on truths in this playful flight.

So let's unravel the universe wide,
With a grin and a bounce, let's take the ride,
For every twist holds joy and fright,
In the grand riddle of the night.

The Playful Dance of Fate

Fate tosses dice with a chuckle and grin,
Playing hopscotch where chaos begins,
Stars align in a rhythmic game,
While comets laugh, never the same.

In every twist, a giggle betrays,
The irony woven in tangled ways,
A whimsical waltz through galaxies bright,
As the universe spins in sheer delight.

Planets tease with their floppy orbits,
While sunbeams tickle the cosmos' limits,
Dancing on suns with a frolicsome flair,
Tickled pink in the cosmic air.

So join the waltz, it's a humorous time,
With fate giving winks, always sublime,
In this playful dance where we partake,
We laugh with the stars for laughter's sake.

The Galactic Comic Strip

Stars in the sky do wink,
Comets giggle, always in sync.
Asteroids dance in a lively jive,
While planets chuckle to just survive.

Black holes munch with a hearty grin,
As supernovas burst, let the fun begin.
The cosmos plays tricks like a jesting fool,
In this grand strip, we're all part of the spool.

Saturn's rings spin tales of glee,
A cosmic dance for you and me.
Meteorites joke as they swiftly race,
In this universe, it's all a wild chase.

Galaxies swirl like clowns on a stage,
Each dark corner hides some witty sage.
So laugh with the stars, join their bright light,
In the cosmic comic, everything feels right.

Irony in the Celestial Realm

In the vast sky where the planets play,
The sun jokes with the moon every day.
Mars, a red punk, throws dusty shade,
While Venus primps, unafraid of the fade.

Gravity pulls with a mischievous shout,
While satellites circle, filled with doubt.
Eclipses tease with a wink and a smile,
Making us ponder, all in their style.

Constellations rearrange their tales,
As stardust laughs and mystery prevails.
The universe winks, a knowing delight,
Irony unfolds in the quiet of night.

Comets skewer thoughts like a cosmic quill,
Creating punchlines with an endless thrill.
So here's to the cosmos, that playful cheer,
In irony's dance, we'll always draw near.

Cosmic Chucklefest

Nebulas puff in vibrant hues,
While quasars flash, sharing some news.
Galactic jesters drift through the void,
In a chucklefest, we're all overjoyed.

Planets collide, oh what a scene,
Bouncing off each other, like a comic routine.
Supernovae laugh with explosive flair,
As they light up the night with dazzling air.

Aliens peek through telescopic eyes,
They ponder our ways, much to their surprise.
Astrological signs throw shade with glee,
In this cosmic circus, we're all meant to be.

Saturn spins tales with its rings so wide,
While black holes chuckle at what they hide.
dancing through stardust, let's join the fest,
In this cosmic comedy, we all are blessed.

The Universe's Witty Repartee

In the void, a conversation begins,
Where stars are the chatter, and black holes grin.
Galaxies converse in swirling delight,
Each word a shimmer, a spark in the night.

Asteroids banter, and comets report,
The sun throws shade, a radiant sport.
With plasma jokes and vacuum puns,
In this repartee, we're all just fun runs.

Planets partake in a round of applause,
For the cosmic humor that gives us cause.
They laugh at the chaos, a sight so grand,
In the universe's chat, we all understand.

Quasars quip, while dark matter nods,
A dance of wit in the lap of the gods.
So let's toast the cosmos, be part of the spree,
In this stellar dialogue, wild and free.

Surreal Whimsy of the Heavens

Stars giggle in the night sky's expanse,
Planets dance in a chaotic romance.
Jupiter's winks and Saturn's sly grins,
Comets swirl, let the giggling begin.

Galaxies twirl like a cosmic ballet,
While black holes munch on space cabaret.
Asteroids chuckle, their orbits they race,
Gravity's pull, it's a funny embrace.

Bright meteors hurl, like a cosmic jest,
Each twinkling light puts the mind to the test.
Nebulas fluff in a colorful spree,
Nature's punchline, so wild and free.

With every tick of the universal clock,
The echoes of laughter in stardust rock.
Whimsy is woven in each stellar thread,
A tapestry tickled, where humor is fed.

Cosmic Nonsense

A quasar wanders, lost and bemused,
While galaxies giggle, whimsically fused.
Pulling pranks from a faraway nook,
Who knew the cosmos could play by its book?

Shooting stars wink, a celestial tease,
Meteor showers that giggle with ease.
Planets in line for a cosmic fair,
Creating bizarre with not a single care.

Dark matter's joke, so dense and quite sly,
It plays hide and seek with a wink to the sky.
Each twirl of the universe, a curly cue,
Beneath it all, a laugh echoes true.

Silly dimensions, so quirky and light,
Tickling particles hide out of sight.
Cosmic jesters in a vacuum's embrace,
To find humor embedded in infinite space.

Earthly Sense

Beneath a blue sky, ants form a queue,
Building vast kingdoms, it's a sight to view.
As clouds roll by, in shapes of delight,
Are they laughing at us from dizzying height?

Pigeons coo secrets as they strut about,
Squirrels throw jokes, with nutty devout.
Flowers bloom brightly, a colorful plot,
Nature conspires to tickle the lot.

In puddles that splatter, we jump with glee,
Riding waves of laughter, full of esprit.
A rainbow cascades, like a smile so wide,
Finding humor in raindrops we've tried to hide.

The sun takes a bow as the day fades away,
With stars that erupt in the dark's cabaret.
All these moments, both silly and grand,
Earth's comedy whispering, hand in hand.

Punchlines in the Dark Matter

In shadows unseen, where comets collide,
Punchlines emerge on interstellar rides.
Quirky encounters of a cosmic kind,
Wit woven deeply, in matter confined.

As black holes gobble the light in retreat,
They chuckle at galaxies passing their seat.
A supernova shrieks as it bursts with cheer,
Knocking socks off of anyone near.

Pulsars tick-tock, with a joke on repeat,
While stardust wisps swirl, oh-so sweet.
Moments like these, we can't help but muse,
How laughter transcends all that we choose.

Cosmic darkness, a backdrop to play,
In the infinite jest, we all find a way.
Punchlines await in the lull of the night,
The universe chortles, our hearts feel the light.

The Universe's Quirky Symphony

In the orchestra of stars, laughter resounds,
Strings pluck and vibrate, in whimsical bounds.
Harmonizing planets groove to the beat,
Echoes of joy in a cosmic retreat.

Winds of asteroids whistle soft tunes,
While cycles of moons spin in merry swoons.
Constellations chuckle, composing their acts,
Creating a melody of cosmic pacts.

Neutron stars thrum with a pulsing jest,
Echoing laughter from galaxies at rest.
The symphony swells, a comedic heart,
Drawing us close with its absurd art.

In the grand concert of the endless skies,
We twirl and we dance, as the stardust flies.
The universe plays on, its quirky refrain,
With each note of humor, we smile through the pain.

www.ingramcontent.com/pod-product-compliance
Lightning Source LLC
Chambersburg PA
CBHW051638160426
43209CB00004B/698